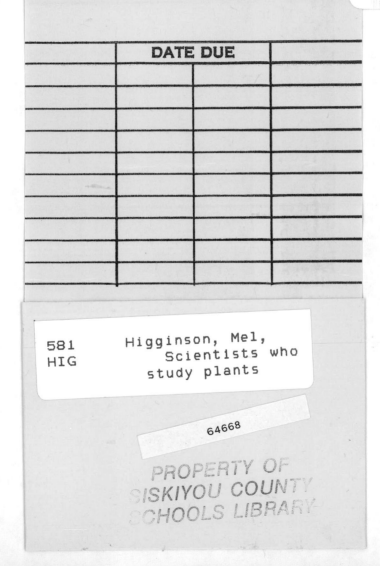

SCIENTISTS WHO STUDY
PLANTS

Mel Higginson

The Rourke Corporation, Inc.
Vero Beach, Florida 32964

Edited by Sandra A. Robinson

PHOTO CREDITS
© Joe Antos, Jr.: cover, pages 4 and 7; © Mel Higginson:
title page, pages 10, 12, 13, 17, 21; courtesy Weyerhaeuser
Company, page 8; courtesy Cargill Seed Division, page 15;
© Tom and Pat Leeson: page 18

Library of Congress Cataloging-in-Publication Data

Higginson, Mel, 1942-
    Scientists who study plants / by Mel Higginson.
        p.   cm. — (Scientists)
    Includes index.
    ISBN 0-86593-373-1
    1. Botanists—Juvenile literature.   2. Botany—Vocational
guidance—Juvenile literature.   [1. Botanists.   2. Botany—
Vocational guidance.   3. Occupations.   4. Vocational guidance.]
I. Title.   II. Series: Higginson, Mel, 1942-   Scientists.
QK50.5.H54   1994
581'.092—dc20   94-6998
                                                          CIP
                                                           AC

Printed in the USA

TABLE OF CONTENTS

SCIENTISTS WHO STUDY PLANTS

Plants grow nearly everywhere on Earth, even on parts of Antarctica. They grow in great numbers and amazing variety. No one knows all about plants — but some people know more than most. They are the **botanists,** the scientists who study plants.

Plant scientists study plants to learn more about how and where they live. They also study ways that plants can be useful to people.

Plant scientists study plants of all kinds in many different kinds of places

WHAT PLANT SCIENTISTS DO

Plant scientists do not all have the same job. What a plant scientist does depends upon that person's special job.

Often, plant scientists collect plants from a wild area. Sometimes they examine plants closely under **microscopes.** Plant scientists preserve plants by mounting them on paper for future study.

Plant scientists raise plants and study their growth. They also study the liquids and chemicals in plants.

These plant scientists are collecting and mapping plants in a study area on Wildcat Mountain in Oregon

KINDS OF PLANT SCIENTISTS

Some plant scientists work just with farm plants, like corn and wheat, or with house plants, like geraniums and pansies. Others work only with trees or with plants that may be used as medicines. Some plant scientists study rain forest or prairie plants.

Certain plant scientists work with plant **fossils.** Fossils are the remains of plants that became **extinct** thousands of years ago.

This plant scientist works in a laboratory for a company that raises trees in huge forests

HERBARIUM OF THE MORTON ARBORETUM

Gentiana crinita Froel.

Lake County, ILLINOIS

East of Zion at th⎯
Nature Cente⎯

WHERE PLANT SCIENTISTS WORK

Most plant scientists spend part of their time outdoors. Their travels lead them into swamps, rain forests, deserts and mountains. They collect, measure, photograph and count plants.

Back at home, plant scientists work in **laboratories,** offices and research stations. Some of a plant scientist's work is done in the library. At the library, the scientist can find out what is already known about plants.

Computers, reference books and microscopes are among the "tools" in the offices and laboratories of plant scientists

The study of plants leads scientists into wild places ...

... and not-so-wild places

THE IMPORTANCE OF PLANT SCIENTISTS

Knowing about plants is important because plants are important to all life. Without plants, animals could not exist. All animals, including people, depend upon plants for food.

Plant scientists help us learn how to grow more and better plants. More crops mean more food, and more trees mean a steady supply of materials for buildings, furniture and paper.

Plant scientists also help find medicines that are made from plants.

This plant scientist works with new varieties of corn and new weedkillers that may help the corn grow better

STUDYING ENDANGERED PLANTS

Certain kinds of plants are rare. Some are **endangered.** That means they are in danger of disappearing, or becoming extinct.

Endangered plants need special attention. Plant scientists plan ways to help save endangered plants. They try to protect plant habitats, the places where these plants grow.

Endangered plants are of special concern in rain forests. Cutting the rain forests has destroyed millions of acres of wild plants.

American plant scientists have a plan to help protect the endangered white-fringed prairie orchid

DISCOVERIES OF PLANT SCIENTISTS

Plant scientists work with great interest and energy. They make new discoveries each day. Plant scientists who prowl in out-of-the-way places discover new kinds of plants.

It's even more important that plant scientists continue to find new ways to use plants as medicines. The bark of the Pacific yew, a shrubby plant of the American Northwest, is useful in battling some cancers.

Medicine made from the bark of Pacific yew trees is used to help treat certain kinds of cancer

LEARNING TO BE A PLANT SCIENTIST

Plant scientists have a background in the study of living things. They also have a background in plants and, often, in certain groups of plants.

People who study plants usually go to college for at least four years. Many plant scientists study even longer.

Plant scientists learn to plan experiments and use laboratory equipment, like electron microscopes.

Plant scientists learn to set up experiments and use a variety of laboratory equipment

CAREERS FOR PLANT SCIENTISTS

Many plant scientists work for local, state and national governments. Governments are interested in the welfare of plants on public lands. They are also interested in finding the plants that might be used as medicines.

Plant scientists work for companies and groups that raise plants, such as seed growers. Plant scientists also work for universities, where they study and teach.

Glossary

botanist (BAHT in ist) — a scientist who studies plants

endangered (en DANE jerd) — in danger of no longer existing; very rare

extinct (ex TINKT) — no longer existing

fossil (FAH suhl) — the ancient remains of plants and animals

laboratory (LAB rah tor ee) — a place where scientists can experiment and test their ideas

microscope (MY kro skope) — a scientific instrument that makes whatever is placed under its lens look larger

INDEX